To Lois

From My Heart to Yours

Love Italene

Selected Poems

by

Italene Gaddis

Copyright © 2012 by Italene Gaddis
All rights reserved.
ISBN: 1479100951
ISBN-13: 978-1479100958

Cover art by Erica Gaddis
Cover design by Erica Gaddis

No part of this publication may be reproduced, stored in or
introduced into a retrieval system, or transmitted, in any form, or by
any means (electronic, mechanical, photocopying, recording, or
otherwise), without the prior written permission of the copyright
owner.

The scanning, uploading, and distribution of this book via the
Internet or via any other means without permission of the publisher
is illegal and punishable by law. Please purchase only authorized
electronic editions, and do not participate in or encourage electronic
piracy of copyrighted materials. Your support of the author's rights
is appreciated.

Weather

It doesn't matter if it is raining,
    and the sky is grey.
There is peace within my mind,
    I'm happy anyway.
For Seattle is my home,
    and I must say,
The weather has no bearing
    on my day.

There is beauty I can see,
    most everywhere.
The other places,
    simply can't compare.
Seattle is the best in every way.
    And the weather has no bearing
on my day.

When you're happy life is really,
    just a game.
You enjoy each season,
    just the same.
There are challenges to meet,
    but I must say.
The weather has no bearing
    . on my day.

I would like to give
    just one word of advice
That word is love
    for it's the key to life
If it lives within your heart
    Then you can say
The weather has no bearing
    on my day.

Weather

It doesn't matter if it is raining
and the sky is grey
or it is just as wide... my mind
it helps anyway
For God's sake my friend
am I much...
The weather, it's no beauty
to my day

there is beauty I can see
most every hour
The birds, flowers
clouds, the rainbow,
Darkness reaches me a way
and the weather has no bearing
to my day

When you're miserable actually
just a part
others feel... about
just the same
These are the things to meet
but I never say
The weather has no bearing
to my day

I would like to give
just one word of advice
That word is love
for it's the key to life
It gives when you need
Then you can say
The weather has no bearing
to my day

Dedication

Without the encouragement and support
of Steven Gaddis these songs and poems
would not be presented for your enjoyment and
encouragement.

Acknowledgements

I want to thank Carl, Pam, and Erica for all the help and encouragement in publishing this book. Carl has really spent a lot of his precious time and expertise putting it together for publication. Telling the story behind the song was his idea as I never would have thought to do that, though I do that in my concerts.

My daughter in law, Pam has encouraged and helped me in many ways and she is my "angel." My granddaughter Erica, has helped in everything I do encouraging me all the way. She is a lady of many talents and my littlest "angel."

How do I put into word how thankful I am to all of them for all the time spent helping me. They took a part of their lives and gave it to me and there is no greater gift they could ever give me.

A special thank you goes to Judy Frohreich for her kindness and help every day that I've been her friend.

Last, but not least I want to thank Jan Curtis the producer of my recordings for all his help and kindness.

Table of Contents

I've Lived the Life	8
Traffic	10
Roads	12
Simple and Sincere	14
They Say	15
Please	16
Dare To Be Different	18
Take Time	19
What is a Woman?	20
Southern Country Gentleman	22
The Texan and the Yellow Rose	24
Happy Song	25
In Your Sight	26
My World	28
Someday	29
Lullaby	30
Father and Child	31
Pollution of the Mind	32
Needed (Someone to Care)	33
My Heavenly Father	34
Play the Game	35
Standing at the Crossroads	36

Day	37
My Thought	37
The Things You Gave To Me	38
Million Dollar Moments	40
I Don't See You with My Eyes	42
Two Little Angels	43
My Son	44
Do You Judge?	40
I Know a Man	46
To Each of My Sons	47
Gift to Me	48
Home	48
Happy Birthday	49
The Riddle Song	50
Thank you to Steven	52
Thank You (Note for Steven)	52
Written for Steven to Steven	53
Damon	54
Guess Who	55
Don't Take Me Back in Time	56
Strength Not Weakness	58
Say and Do It Now	59

Life	59
Alone Again	60
Do It	61
My Day	62
The Spirit	63
Yesterday is Dead	63
Thank you to All I Love	64
A Farewell to Larry and Laurie	65
The Only Way (to live)	66
All Brothers and Sisters	67
Sister of the Universe	68
We	69
The Rebel	70
Love is the Answer	72
The Encouragement Song	73
If You Are Grateful	74
In This World	75
Life, the Question	76
Life, the Answer	78
Father	79
Thank You	80
Child of God	82

I've Lived the Life

I've lived the life of
    a child in the country,
Roaming the fields
    so happy and free.
I've lived the life of
    a teen in the city,
Dreaming and wondering
    what life held for me.

I've lived the life of
    a wife and a mother.
I've lived the life of
    a woman in love.
I played with my children
    and pleased my husband,
I didn't know what
    the world was made of.

I've lived the life of
    a woman in business,
Competing with men
    and women it's true.
I know what it's like to
    make all the money,
and pay the bills
    when they come due.

Now I'm living the life
   of a woman in music.
Singing my songs from
   my heart and soul.
In hopes I can show you
   that love is the answer.
From my heart to your heart
   that is my goal.

I've Lived the Life

The highlights of my life are all in this poem and it's all true. It's also in the sequence of what happened. When I say I didn't know what the world was made of I truly didn't but I had to learn. So I did. Believe me anyone can change, because believe me I know how much of a change I had to make in my life. I'm grateful and thankful for each and every experience. They have taught me many things.

Traffic

I wake up in the morning
   and turn on the radio,
To listen to the traffic
   and figure out which way to go.
But as I start to listen
   what I always seem to hear,
The bridges are a parking lot
   you can't get there from here.

I-5 's jammed north bound
   and south bound is a mess,
The Ballard bridge is open
   Highway 99 's in distress.
405's on-ramps
   are backing up again,
To the Boeing plant in Everett
   and my nightmare just begins.

I get into my car
   I know the freeway's bad,
The side roads are clogged up
   and the boss is getting mad.
The worker's same excuse is
   day after day you know,
" I'm late again to work boss
   for the traffic was so slow."

Now I'm sitting in the traffic
   wondering what to do,
The freeway looks like a parking lot
   But wait now I'm telling you.

I think I've found the answer
    though some folks think I'm mad,
my car is now my office,
    and the commute is not half bad.

As I'm sitting on the freeway
    I make a call or two,
Fax into my first appointment
    the papers that are due.
Turn on my computer
    to watch a trade and soon,
I'll be adding a television
    so I can watch the soaps at noon.

I think I've really licked it
    commuting around Puget Sound.
I only have one worry
    while I'm sitting around.
The Department of Transportation
    may wonder by and see,
Me using up their freeway
    and charge office rent to me.

Traffic

I didn't want to write this song because I thought it might be
negative. But you can take a negative and make a positive
out of it. That's what I set out to do with this song. Though
the freeways may be different where you live, you pretty
well understand this is the way it goes.

Roads

Every road we travel
   there's a lesson to be learned,
And a new adventure
   with each page of life we turn.
Every day is a new beginning
   in this space we know as time,
As for me I know there'll be
   another song to rhyme.

Roads go here, roads go there,
   which one will you choose?
Sometimes we take the wrong one,
   and then we're sure to lose.
But wait, it's not a loss
   if it helps to make us grow,
Each experience helps to teach us
   things we need to know.

As you travel down the road of life
   I hope that you will find,
Lots of love and happiness
   and true piece of mind.
But if for any reason
   you're not where you want to be,
Then change directions 'till you find
   the road to set you free.

Roads are just a symbol
   of all of life you see.
Roads are just a symbol
   of life's diversity.

Roads

I used to drive from 50 to 300 miles a day making a living for my family. Going away from home was very difficult. I usually did so at a very slow speed. Coming back I had to watch that I didn't go over the speed limit. There were times I'd look down and I was doing 80 going home. Then a trucker would blink his lights and I would realize I'd better slow down, which I would do so I wouldn't get at ticket. I only got one ticket in my life and I said I'd never get another. So far at 87 I've kept that promise. If it says 25, that's what I go. If it says 55, that's what I go.

I've had a lot of the young people ask me for "Roads" because it's about life. If you're living life, this poem pretty well explains the choices you have.

Simple and Sincere

The things my mother taught me
    have helped along the way,
But the most important things she taught
    I remember every day.
She would hold me close and whisper,
    "Now listen to me dear,
Don't complicate your life
    keep it simple and sincere. "

She would say, "Remember
    and always be yourself,
No matter how you try
    you can't be someone else.
Each one of us is special
    like no one else that's here,
Don't complicate your life
    keep it simple and sincere. "

Each person has a gift
    that's given to be used,
To make the world a better place
    Believe me you can't lose.
If you just give it all you've got
    and remember while you're here,
Don't complicate your life
    keep it simple and sincere.

They Say

They say if you are young
    the world belongs to you.
Young or old it matters not
    it's all in what you do.

They say that I could pass
    for forty or forty-five.
I've been there and it was great
    you can see that I've survived.

Age is just a number
    Take a tip from me.
I'll be just as happy
    when I say I'm ninety-three.

They say that if by forty
    you haven't made your mark.
You may as well lay down and die
    It's just too late to start.

I've never met this fellow
    you keep referring to,
and with a name as strange as they
    I hope I never do.

Please

First you please your parents,
   Then when you are grown
you try to please the one
   you've chosen for your own.
Very soon the children come
   and you please them one by one
Trying hard to make a house a home.

You go to church on Sunday
   just to please the lord.
You go to work on Monday
   you're working very hard,
Just to please the boss
   so you can draw your pay,
On and On it goes, day after day.

Is all this pleasing, pleasing you?
   Are you happy in all the things you do?
There's a question in my mind,
   Tell me please if you don't mind,
Is all this pleasing, pleasing you?

You try to please your family
   You try to please your friends.
Do you ever wonder, will it ever end?
   You're always busy pleasing everybody else,
Remember, you've got to please yourself.

Please

I was on my way over to Carl's house and I was thinking of my life and how we often go through life trying to please everyone. I've heard people say, "I have the please disease." Well, I've had it all my life and it's something I will probably never correct.

Although Father gave me this poem in 10 minutes and He's given me so many lessons and advice on things, this pleasing is something I can't seem to change in myself. It seems my subconscious says," If you please other people then you can be happy." But the reality of it is, if you are doing what you enjoy doing, that happiness flows to others. If you are doing what you don't like to do so does that unhappiness.

Dare To Be Different

Dare to be different,
   dare to be you.
You were born,
  to give the world something new.
Guard against being
 anyone's fool,
Always live by
 the golden rule.

There are those who will tell you,
   when to walk or to run.
They're seeking power,
  to control everyone.
Be your own person,
   do things your way.
And always remember,
   these words that I say.

Life is a challenge,
   life is a game.
People are like flowers,
   no two are the same.
They grow and they bloom,
   each in their own time.
So always keep trying,
   and remember this rhyme.

The road you travel
    to the left or the right,
They are as different
    as day is from night.
Your choice determines
    whether you win or lose.
Positive or negative
    which one will you choose.

Take Time

As I was all alone
    in quiet meditation,
Thinking of my place
    in all of God's creation.
I realized I may be
    running far too fast.
I must slow down
    and make each moment last.
For there are those around me
    who really may not know,
How much they mean to me
    if I didn't let it show.

What is a Woman?

A woman is a lady,
    a girl and a child.
She can be gentle,
    or she can be wild.
She can be a mother,
    a wife and a friend.
A woman is someone,
    on whom to depend.

Don't tell me woman,
    is weaker than man.
She was created equal,
    according to plan.
Man has an ego,
    that says dominate.
Believe me, both woman
    and man can be great.

A woman is a giver,
    but she loves to receive.
Don't dominate her or you'll
    force her to leave.
She grows on love and
    without it she dies.
She lives on truth,
    don't tell her lies.

If you can't love her,
   then leave her alone.
Don't be possessive,
   her soul is her own.
She will love and cherish,
   if you'll do the same.
It takes true commitment,
   for her to remain.

What is a Woman?

     I had a friend who asked me the question, "What is a woman?" My thought was, "That's the dumbest thing I've ever been asked." My mother taught me that I can think different things, but be careful what I say because I can't take it back. But my answer to my friend was, "I don't know, I just am one." She was writing a book to motivate women to do what they want to do and I did open my mouth and said something I wished I hadn't. She said she wanted to motivate women. I said, "Well if they have to pay the bills that will motivate them." I know about paying the bills. This is just my explanation of what a woman is.

  When I perform this song, I like to explain this particular verse

She can be gentle,
  or she can be wild.

I am definitely a gentle woman, but if you mess with my family then you will see my wild side. That's what I call a real woman. She is gentle but she is strong. And that's also what I call a real man. He is gentle but he is strong.

Southern Country Gentleman

There are men and gentlemen,
    there are good old boys.
Some of them are quiet,
    some make lots of noise.
Let me tell you here and now
    whether short or tall.
A southern country gentleman
    is the finest man of all.

He likes to sing, he likes to talk.
    If he takes you for a walk,
He will steal a kiss if he can.
    He's just himself and nothing more.
Believe me ladies you'll adore,
    A southern country gentleman.

I am sure you have heard,
    once he's given you his word
Then he offers you his hand.
    That's his bond and you can bet,
That you never will forget,
    A southern country gentleman.

There's a place in Texas so they say,
    a quiet and peaceful hide-away,
And they call in Garland Bend.
    All your cares you will forget,
If you go there you'll be met by
    A southern country gentleman

Southern Country Gentleman

I guess this is what I call a real man. They are just themselves and nothing more. When they give you their word, you can depend on it. It's written in stone. You can depend on them in every shape and form. I married one. He was from Kentucky. But I did not write this for him.

 I was outside of Seattle at the Evergreen State Fair to do a concert and there was a young man working there. I saw the stage that I was going to be entertaining on and I wanted to get close to it so I wouldn't have a long way to walk. I drove up and rolled my window down and said, "I'm going to be performing on that stage, where can I park."

He said, "You can park right here." Then he began to sing. When he walked away I wrote Southern Country Gentleman. Then the last verse was added for a gentleman that I knew. Garland was his last name.

When I recorded the song I had to ask him if I could use his name and he said, "You can include me in anything you do Italene."

The Texan and the Yellow Rose

A tall Texas gentleman
    came riding into town.
He was asking questions
    and looking all around.

He said, "I had a yellow rose
    a long, long time ago.
I wonder where she is today,
    does anybody know?"

I looked into the Texan's eyes
    he could not hide the truth.
The love was just as strong today
    as it had been in his youth.

I said, "I know the Yellow rose,
    she is just as fair today
As she was when you knew her,
    before you went away."

Though many years had come and gone
    I knew when their eyes met,
The feeling deep within their hearts
    they never would forget .

I do not know the ending
    to the story I have told.
But I do know the Texan
    found his Yellow Rose.

The Texan and the Yellow Rose

That's a true story that actually took place. A young man fell in love with a lady and they had gone their separate ways. Many years had gone by and they hadn't seen each other. Then they met again and were united. This was written for them.

Happy Song

It seems there is a reason
    for each and every season.
They all have beauty plain to see,
It doesn't matter whether
    it's clear or stormy weather,
You can sing a happy song like me.

If you will look around you
    at the beauty that surrounds you,
It's there if you will take the time to see.
So much to give you pleasure,
    Things that you could treasure,
Along with all the happy memories.

But if money is what you're after,
    you'll find very little laughter.
The song will not be happy that you sing.
You will lose the touch of magic
    and it really is quite tragic,
You will miss the joy that simple things can bring.

In Your Sight

You're oh so quick to criticize
    the things I say and do.
Finding fault comes easy
    when I'm not pleasing you.
Where are the compliments
    when I do something right?
It's very clear to me
    I'm half a person in your sight.

I never knew anyone
    with no faults at all.
In this life we stumble
    and sometimes we fall.
No one is perfect
    no one is always right.
It's very clear to me
    I'm half a person in your sight.

The only time my boss
    seems to notice me.
Is when I make an error,
    why can't he ever see?
Any of the good I do
    never comes to light.
It's very clear to me
    I'm half a person in his sight.

As you go through life
   I hope you will recall,
It's important to acknowledge
   the good that's in us all.
If you can only see the left
   and cannot see the right,
You are only half a person
   for that is all that's in your sight.

In Your Sight

You can do a job for someone and do an excellent job and there is no conversation between the boss and you. However, if you make a mistake he's got time to talk to you. That just never seemed quite right to me.

Actually I said right out loud, "I think if you only acknowledge the negative and not the positive you're only half a person." But it wouldn't be nice to call a person a half a person so I turned it around from the opposite angle. I wrote it so the way the boss saw me was as being half a person. Until the last verse and then I sock it to them.

My World

I will paint my world
   with sunshine every day.
I will have the flowers
   blooming on my way.
I will find the dream
   others never found.
With laughter and music
   to always be around.

I will paint my world
   with colors oh so bright,
Where darkness cannot enter
   even in the night.
Then I will have the moon
   and stars above,
To light my way for pleasure
   with my love.

I tried so hard to make
   this dream come true.
Each day I would make
   my vow anew.
And promise myself I would know success,
   and achieve the thing I sought for-
Happiness.

Try if you will and make your dream come true.
   I never could or never would discourage you.
Who can say, maybe you will win.
   If you can try and try and try again.

Someday

I pick up the phone and I hear your voice.
You tell me you love me and you've made a choice.
You say to be patient, Someday you'll be free.
You promise that Someday you will be with me.

I thought there were only seven days in a week.
I've never heard of this day of which you speak.
I want to believe you so please tell me dear.
When will this Someday you refer to be here?

You ask me to meet you tonight all alone.
We'll talk about Someday when you'll be my own.
I love all the promises that you make to me.
But please tell me, when will this Someday be.

Is it some special holiday I've not heard about?
Does it come very often? I've got to find out.
I'm sure there are others like me that don't know
About this special Someday when everything is go.

Someday

     This was written for a lady who kept thinking that someday everything would be ok and she would be married and everything would be ... Kind of like me when I wrote "My World" I thought I'd have the perfect world. I started to write "Someday" from her viewpoint because she would talk a lot on the phone with him. He'd say someday we'll be together. She thought they'd be married. Then while I was writing this song, I came to a stop light and I turned back into me. That's when I realized there isn't any someday. There are only 7 days in week. This poem is actually part someone else's point of view and the second verse is me. There isn't any someday. You might think about this when someone tells you someday.

Lullaby

This is a lullaby.
   This is a song.
Listen to me and
   before very long,
Your mind will drift
   setting your sprit free.
 This is a lullaby.
   Listen to me.

This is a picture
   you paint in your mind.
Leaving all tension
   and worries behind.
The flowers are blooming,
   perfume fills the air.
Springtime is showing
   her beauty so fair.

The sun is shining,
   you feel a cool breeze.
The grass is so soft,
   as you lay 'neath the trees.
As you look up,
   you see a blue sky.
White cotton clouds
   slowly drift by.

You hear the birds,
   as they sing you their song.
This is the place
   where you belong.

Lullaby

I wrote this to relax my sister who was dying of lung cancer. I did not know until my son said to me after he read it, "Mother it's filled with meditation imagery." I didn't know what he meant, but once he explained that to me I couldn't explain how I'd chosen those words except that all the things that I write are given to me. When I write something, the way I write it is the way I feel about it when I write it. It is almost as though I'm just writing them down. I think all of my songs and poems are given to me by my Heavenly Father.

Father and Child

Your father that gave you life
    now lives on in you.
There is a part of you in him
    and a part of him in you.
And though you cannot
    see him now,
It does not mean
    he's gone.
For the part of him you knew
    is alive and still lives on.
Someday we'll understand
    the reason for it all.
Until then each of us
    must answer to the call.
As we were born alone,
    so must we go the same.
We came bringing nothing,
    we leave behind a name.

Pollution of the Mind

They tell us of pollution
    In the air and in the sea.
We're destroying our environment
    And also you and me.

There is another poison
    Of a different kind.
It is called
    Pollution of the mind.

The newspapers and magazines
    Could be a delight.
If they would present,
    The positive side of life.

The music on the radio
    Could lift our spirit high.
If the songs they played,
    Gave a message to live by.

The television set we watch
    Could teach us how to live.
Showing us the beauty
    And what it's like to give.

Needed (Someone to Care)

Have you ever walked the street at night
    and felt the hurt inside,
Of the people that you pass
    who have lost all hope and pride?

How could you help but wonder
    is there something I can do?
And perhaps if things were different
    that might be me or you.

Did you stop to talk or listen
    or did you just hurry by,
Trying not to notice
    or even wonder why?

In this land of plenty
    with its riches oh so rare
It's really difficult to find
    someone who really cares.

My Heavenly Father

My Father is there.
He hears every prayer.
I am His own.
I am never alone.

When I wake up each morning,
I thank Him for my rest.
I ask Him to watch over me
And help me do my best.

When the day is done,
I thank Him for my day.
Each and every blessing
That He has sent my way.

My Heavenly Father

My father left my mother with four children to raise
when I was two. I was taught that I didn't have an earthly
father but I did have a Heavenly one and He would be
with me every moment of my life. I would never be alone.
He would always be there if I needed Him and that has
made my life so much better because of that teaching.

There are so many people in this world that feel they
have no one that cares. I've always known I was loved and
cared about. Maybe that's why I never felt alone. I knew
my Heavenly Father loved me. I knew my mother loved
me. I knew that my brothers loved me, my sister loved
me. There are others who do not have that.

Play the Game

I don't understand the word lonely,
    I don't think I've ever been blue.
I've too many friends to be lonely,
    and not enough time to be blue.

This life is a gamble we're living,
    and I think we're all just the same.
Let me advise you if you hope to win,
    you've got to join in the game.

Thinking of course is important,
    but it's action that gets the job done.
So if there is something you want to do,
    I do hope that you have begun.

Standing at the Crossroads

Standing at the crossroads
  wondering which way to go,
Left or right or straight ahead
  down the same old road I know.

There are so many questions
  running through my mind,
How do I make a choice
  not knowing what I'll find.

There is no way of knowing
  there is no guarantee,
We just know our lessons
  will shape our destiny.

There is no way of knowing
  what's around the bend,
No one has the answers
  of how the road will end.

Standing at the Crossroads

I think we've all been there. I know I have been many
times in my life. Choosing which way to go. But you know
sometimes we need to stand at the crossroad and take a
look at our life and see if we're going on the road we want
to or do we take the off ramp.

Day

I don't regard one day above another.
Each one is special in this life we live.
With every sunrise there's a new beginning
Another chance for us to love and give.

This is our time of freedom.
There are things that we must do.
The road I'm walking now
Is beautiful and new.

Each day we live is brighter
Than the day before.
How wonderful it is to see
What each one has in store.

My Thought

Our planet is very fragile.
Yes, Earth is very small.
We as human beings are
Brothers and sisters all.

Though we may think differently
We really are the same,
We all believe in a Maker
Though we call him different names.

Now does it really matter?
Isn't love what it's all about?
And if we put the loving first
Then we can work things out.

The Things You Gave To Me

You say that I deserve someone
  to give me many things.
Don't you know there's more to give
  than gold and diamond rings?
You gave to me your arms
  to hold me close to you.
And money cannot buy
  a pair of eyes so blue.
Where on sale can I find
  a heart so kind and true?
My Darling, all these things you gave me
  when you said, "I do."

The things that money cannot buy,
  are much more precious, dear.
You cannot buy a blue sky,
  when the sunshine won't appear.
Who would want to live alone,
  and live in luxury?
What good are precious jewels,
  if dreams can never be.
You say I only have your love
  that's enough for me.
I would not take a million,
  for the things you gave to me.

To know I will possess your heart
    until the day I die,
Means more to me than all the things,
    that gold could ever buy.
The happiness that we have shared,
    so very few have known.
A contented mind you also gave,
    For I know you are mine alone.
There is no end to all the gifts,
    You gave so willingly.
I could never tell you all
    the things you gave to me.

The Things You Gave to Me

I wrote this for my husband because after ten years of
married life he became ill and could no longer work. He had
a real problem with it. He would often say to me, "You
deserve someone to give you many things." Well, in this
poem I tried to reveal to him that things don't make you
happy and there are other things that money can't buy. I'm
grateful that I valued those things more than what money
could buy.

Million Dollar Moments

I had a loving Mother
    she gave so much to me.
Those million dollar moments
    live in my memories.
She always knew just what to do
    to make my world seem bright.
Her million dollar moments
    made it right.

Million dollar moments
    the story of my life.
Million dollar moments
    when I became his wife.
He was the one I wanted
    to always hold me tight.
He gave me million dollar moments
    in the night.

Million dollar moments
    I count them one by one.
Million dollar moments
    with my daughter and my sons.
They are my very world
    I hope they can see.
What those million dollar moments
    mean to me.

Million dollar moments
    that I spent with a baby.
Time went by so quickly,
    now she is a lady.
When we are together
    she's an angel in my eyes.
Million dollar moments
    come alive.

There was a little boy
    who came to live a while.
I recall his laughter,
    I recall his smile.
Though our time together
    was only now and then,
There were million dollar moments
    spent with him.

Million dollar moments
    happen every day.
Cherish and enjoy them
    before they slip away.

Million Dollar Moments

This is the way that I feel when I remember my mother, my sons, my daughter-in-law, my granddaughter and my grandson. I think million dollar moments are something each person makes when they live their life and they should try quite deliberately to make a lot of million dollar moments.

I Don't See You with My Eyes

The years have swiftly passed,
    Time has taken its toll.
According to the number,
    you and I are growing old.
There is something you should know,
    that's been true right from the start.
I don't see you with my eyes,
    I see you with my heart.

They say that love is blind,
    on that I will agree.
For when I look at you,
    I don't see what others see.
I look into your soul,
    to a kind and loving part.
I don't see you with my eyes,
    I see you with my heart.

You are young and you are pretty,
    with a flower in your hair.
And when you speak you reassure me,
    telling me how much you care.
I know your love protects me,
    even when we're far apart.
I don't see you with my eyes,
    I see you with my heart.

I am speaking of you Mother,
    My angel here on earth.
I know that you have loved me,
    Since the moment of my birth.
This song is just for you,
    With a message to impart.
I don't see you with my eyes,
    I see you with my heart.

I Don't See You with My Eyes

    I wrote that poem when my mother was 98 years old. She was at a birthday party and she was asked what it was like to be old and she said, "Well, I'm not old yet."
    I got up out of bed and wrote this in 10 minutes which is usually what it takes to write what I feel. I think that when we love someone we do not really see them the way they are, and my wish, if I had one, is that the world could see people with their hearts and not just their eyes.

Two Little Angels

Two little angels to live and to hold.
Two little angels worth more than gold.
Two little angels to brighten my world.
One is a boy, one is a girl.

The treasures I have are worth more than gold.
The memories they gave me will never grow old.
I know they were sent from Heaven above.
Two little angels with hearts filled with love.

My Son

I wrote this for you son
    in hopes to convey,
A message of love
    though I really must say.
Words are so useless
    to express how I feel,
For my love for you
    I could never reveal.

You were loved and wanted
    from the time I knew,
You've been loved each
    and every year through.
As a baby I cared for
    and enjoyed you so,
As a little boy I told you
    all you wanted to know.

As a young man I shared
    your hopes and dreams
I longed to give you
    oh, so many things.
Even though I could not
    give all you desired,
I gave all I could
    and you were so admired.

Just because you're a man
    and on your own,
Doesn't mean you will
    ever be alone.
For my love lives on
    through the years.
I will always be concerned
    for your hopes and fears.

When one cares for someone
    as I have for you,
I will never reach the point
    where I feel I'm through.
For my love
    truly knows no end,
I am one person
    you can truly call friend.

My Son

I wrote this for my oldest son, Carl, when he went
away to college. You think, "Only yesterday he was just a
little boy and now my son's a man." This is the way any
mother who loves her son would want to give her son a
poem that expresses these feelings. You are the best friend
they will ever have or should be the best friend.

I Know a Man

I know a man
 that lives each day
Helping others along the way.

I know a man
 that's worthy of
Your respect, your trust, and love.

I know a man
 with a heart of love
For his brothers and sisters
 and God above.

Do You Judge

Do you judge a man
 by the cut of his hair and the color of his skin?
Do you judge a man by the clothes that he wears
 without knowing the man within?

Do You Judge

Just 4 lines, but isn't that enough. I was at a party and an older person, a man, came up to me and said in a negative tone, "Look at that kid over there with the long hair."

You know he didn't even know the young man. I knew the young man and I knew he was in college and was doing his very best to do well and do what he could to be of help to the world. I walked away and wrote the poem.

To Each of My Sons

My son you owe me nothing,
But I am indebted to you.
For all the happy memories,
And the love you gave me.

You let me share so many things,
I want to thank you now.
There is no way I can repay,
Though I wish I could somehow.

To Each of My Sons

I do not feel that my children owe me anything because having them has been a blessing. I have wanted two sons from the time I was very very young. Even before I could have children, I knew I wanted two sons.

I asked my husband when we got married. I said I wanted two sons. He said he wanted a couple of girls. I said, "Well I will have the boys, and you can have the girls." My sister had two girls. I felt that I could be a better mother to sons. I've felt that way since I was a child.

Gift to Me

I would like to thank you for your love
    and kind and tender ways.
For all the many things you've done
    through all these many days.
To me it's been a gift supreme
    and one that I shall treasure.
Looking back in memory
    will give me so much pleasure.
You took a part of your life
    and gave it willingly.
I just wanted you to know
    there is no greater gift to me.

Home

I wandered in a world today
    like I've never known,
For there was beauty everywhere
    and there was a place called home.

At first I thought it was a house
    but as I walked through the door,
When I began to look around
    I could see it was much more.

There was love and kindness
    and it was plain to see,
There was understanding, too
    in this home of tranquility.

Happy Birthday

The day my son was born
And he began his life,
I wished for someone just like you
To be his princess and his wife.

I knew somewhere you waited,
I told him it would be.
I knew that you would bring
Happiness to him and me.

How could I help but love you,
For you care about my son.
I have loved and waited for you
Since the day his life begun.

I, his Mother, was his first love
But to make his life complete,
I knew that he must find
Someone like you so kind and sweet.

I just wanted so to thank you
And I take this special way,
To send my love and best wishes
To you on your birthday.

The Riddle Song

She's a wife and she's a Mother,
    I've never known another quite like her.
She's a girl and she's a lady.
    She never does say maybe.
It's "yes or no" she knows her mind for sure.

She's as gentle as a kitten,
    but she's a woman made of steel.
Don't know what I'd do without her,
    there is nothing fake about her.
She's an Angel and she's real.

I can tell you that I love her,
    There's no woman that's above her.
In my mind she's number One,
    I know that I've been blessed.
You'll understand when I confess.
    The lady is married to my son.

The Riddle Song

My car needed to have a part so the mechanic told me when I took it in for an oil change. He said, "Italene I'm going to have to order your part so you're going to have to rent a car.

I said, "Ok."

He took me home. I called Carl ,my older son, to tell him. I said, " I guess I'm going to have to rent a car because they didn't have a part they needed to fix it."

He said why don't I come and get you and you can use my car. His car was an older car and as a matter of fact they had bought a new car a couple of weeks before. He said we can get along with one car and you can use mine until you get yours fixed and then you can bring it back. I'll come and get you and you can have dinner.

My daughter-in-law is a wonderful cook and I looked forward to that. So after dinner I said give me the car keys and I'll be going. My daughter-in-law stood up and said "You're not taking Carl's car." She walked over to where they kept the car keys and got the keys to her brand new car and came back and said, "You're taking mine."

On the way home I wrote this song. I couldn't think of what to name it. Finally I said this is a riddle, so that is what I named it. When I sing this song I always say you're not going to know who I'm singing about until the end.

Thank you to Steven

I'd like for you to know
    I appreciate your way,
Of showing that you care
    each and every day.
The things you say,
    the things you do,
They mean so much
    coming from you.

The encouragement
    you've given me,
Has pushed me forward
    and set me free.
To try and make
    my dreams come true,
This is my way
    to thank you.

Thank You (Note for Steven)

Thank you for believing in me
    and for your help each day.
For all the encouragement
    you give along the way.
Thank you for the gifts you give
    and all the things you do
That make my life worth living
    all because of you.

Written for Steven to Steven

Please be good to Steven
    because I love him so.
Don't do anything to hurt him
    he means so much to me you know.

Whether he succeeds or fails
    I feel depends on me
for I'm the one who taught him
    most of his philosophy.

If you love and care about me
    as you often say you do.
Then please be good to Steven
    and make his dreams come true.

There are many ways to make a point
    I hope that you will see.
By being good to Steven
    you are being good to me.

Damon

Damon was a special boy
　　with a heart so full of love.
I called him my angel
　　sent down from God above.

He would greet me with a smile
　　and a twinkle in his eyes.
He called my name as though
　　it was some special prize.

We laughed and talked
　　We played and walked
This special little boy and I.
　　He was full of questions,
Like how and when and why.

I would tell him stories
　　just the way I told his dad.
You see he was the son
　　of the little boy I had.

Damon was a special boy.
　　with a heart so full of love.
Now he is an angel.
　　returned to God above.

We've been taught we must accept
    things that we cannot change.
But I can tell you truthfully,
    I'll never be the same.

We laughed and talked
    We played and walked
This little boy and I.
    I'm the one with questions now
My mind keeps asking, why.

Guess Who

I know someone that's pretty
    She is gentle and so kind.
She does not hesitate
    to tell you what's on her mind.

She will make you think of things
    you never thought before.
I can tell you here and now
    she is someone I adore.

She can accomplish more
    than anyone I know.
I'm sure that you can tell
    I truly love her so.

The person I've described
    is truly one of a kind.
She's my granddaughter
    and is always pleasant on my mind.

Don't Take Me Back in Time

You take me with you
    when you sing about a broken heart,
Bringing back the memories
    that make the teardrops start.
You take away the sunshine with your sad refrain
    you take me back in time renewing all the pain.

Please don't take me back in time.
    Take me to tomorrow.
Sing your song and take away yesterday's sorrow.
    Tell me things I've never heard,
About places I've not been.
    But please don't take me back in time
I don't want to hurt again.

Take me to tomorrow,
    tell me things to be,
That all my hopes and dreams will become reality.
    Take me with you as you sing
Your songs in rhyme.
    All I ask is please
Don't take me back in time.

Please don't take me back in time,
    Take me to tomorrow.
Sing your song and take away yesterday's sorrow.
    Tell me things I've never heard
About places I've not been.
    But please don't take me back in time
I don't want to hurt again.

Don't Take Me Back in Time

This is a poem/song written to a country singer who writes and sings hurting songs. What they do is take you back in time and renew all the pain. I went to do a concert on Orcas Island and stayed in a bed and breakfast. The house was the vintage of the 30s or 40s. The hot water faucet was on the left and the cold water faucet was on the right and you had to use a stopper. It certainly took me back in time. I didn't want to be taken back in time.

At that time I was making my cds and recording my songs. I didn't want to go back in time. I wanted to see what lay ahead and all the dreams that I was now beginning to dream of what my life could be and how I could encourage others to make their lives better and give them something positive to think about.

Strength Not Weakness

If I cannot come to you with strength,
    I will not come with weakness.
If I cannot give, I will not take.
    You have problems of your own,
I would never add mine to them.
    There's no reason you should
pay for my mistake.

I'm a friend of yours and I believe,
    you are a friend of mine.
I hope our friendship always will remain.
    I'll do anything I can to help you,
You can count on me.
    But if I cannot bring you sunshine
I will not bring you rain.

Strength Not Weakness

This is just the way I personally feel. I don't say others should feel this way. I try to give others strength and not come with weakness. I usually kept my weakness to myself whether that's good or bad I'm not sure, but it's the way I feel. I never dictate what someone else should do, but I like to be a friend and I like to bring happiness and positiveness to people. We have so much of the other that is thrust upon us that I try not to burden others with my problems. I feel they have enough of their own.

Say and Do It Now

We don't know why life passes by
    it's gone before we know it.
We become upset
    and we regret our love, we didn't show it.

Please do not wait 'til it's too late
    say It now and don't delay.
It does no good to say,
    "I should have said it
yesterday."

So, as you live
    just try to give someone a little pleasure.
You will find true peace of mind
    with memories to treasure.

Life

Life is like a puzzle
    and each piece we put in place
Represents the days we live
    in this time and space.
Once the piece has been put down
    there is nothing we can do.
Past is past and yesterday
    cannot be lived anew.

Alone Again

Alone again
   with my memories of you.
Alone again
   dreaming dreams that can't come true.
That's when I miss you most
   and long to hold you close
When I'm alone again.

I'm still living my life
   just the way I did before.
When I'm busy I can hide
   what I'm longing for.
But when the day is over
   and I go home once more,
Things are oh so different
   when I close the door.

I realize and face reality
   when day is here.
Life goes on and things
   in my mind are clear.
But when the evening shadows fall
   and I go home at night.
I know what to expect
   when I turn out the light.

Alone again
    with my memories of you.
Alone again
    dreaming dreams that can't come true
That's when I miss you most
    and long to hold you close
When I'm alone again.

Alone Again

I wrote this after my husband passed away. My son made a statement that, "Mother I will get you a counselor if you feel you want me to." But the only counselor I've ever had is my Father in Heaven and so I said no I am fine. I went home and wrote this. I was fine during day when I was busy. You see I guess I've always been a workaholic. I think that's what you call it. When I'm busy, I'm concentrating on what I'm doing until I'm alone again.

Do It

If there is something we should do.
Let's do it.

Put our minds and muscles to it.
Join hands and pursue it.
Together we can win.

There are those who hesitate
They make excuses and they wait.
They hem and haw 'till it's too late.
They never do begin.

My Day

As I wake up each morning,
    you are the first thing that I see.
I tell you how I love you
    while I drink my cup of tea.
I hurry out the door,
    wishing you a pleasant day.
My mind then turns to things
    that I must do and say.
All day long I concentrate
    on the job at hand.
Trying not to think of you
    I'm sure you understand.
Once again when I come home
    and open up the door.
I know you will be waiting there.
    I'll see your face once more.
So each day will begin
    and also end the same.
For I am only talking to
    a picture in a frame.

My Day

This was written in about 5 min. Normally I write my poems in about 10 min. It's a feeling I have and I seldom change a word. I didn't mean to time it but I picked up my pen, the clock was there with the picture. It was written for my Grandson. We only got to have him 9 years and he was a joy. I really had not felt a loss in my life that was this hurtful until we lost him as a result of an automobile accident.

The Spirit

The spirit never ages
    It always stays the same,
From youth 'till when we're older
    through all time it will remain.
The physical may alter,
    changes that are plain to see,
The spirit is what counts
    that is really you and me.
So remember what's important
    is the spirit we possess,
It's in the image of our Father,
    we're his children nothing less.

Yesterday is Dead

We cannot bring one moment back
    no matter how we try.
Don't waste your thoughts on yesterday
    and sit and wonder why.

Yesterday can take away
    your today and your tomorrow.
Don't let It steal your happiness
    and leave you only sorrow.

You know today is now, alive,
    and yesterday is dead.
We know not what tomorrow brings,
    live today, is what I've said.

Thank you to All I Love

How can I ever thank you
    for the many things you give,
Not only for today
    but every day I live.

For the joy and happiness
    is beyond all measure,
Not only for the moment
    but memories to treasure.

It seems our time together
    is so swiftly gone,
But it leaves sweet memories
    in our mind to linger on.

I love you so, I'm sure you know
    It's always hard to part,
So until I hold you in my arms
    I'll hold you in my heart.

A Farewell to Larry and Laurie

We'll remember all the things
  you taught us through the years.
You were there to share our joy
  and to share our tears.
Helping us to understand,
  lending us a helping hand
Gently you calmed our fears.

There will always be a special place
  in our hearts for you.
We'll recall the gentleness and
  kindness that is you.
When we cannot see your face
  time will not erase
Our memories of you.

So as you live your life
  we wish you happiness.
Even though we'll miss you
  we'll love you none the less.
It's our hope and so we pray
  our path will cross along the way.
Until then we ask the Lord to bless.

The Only Way (to live)

There are things I do not know,
    Where I come from, where I go,
It's here and now that matters though -
    The only way to live.

Questions running through my mind,
    Answers I may never find,
Still I know that being kind -
    The only way to live.

Reaching out a helping hand,
    Spreading love through all the land,
This I know and understand -
    The only way to live.

In this life we all must share,
    If you're needed, just be there,
Let others know how much you care -
    The only way to live.

These are words I had to say.
    So I wrote this song today,
Spread your love along the way -
    The only way to live.

The Only Way to Live

I had performed a concert where there were some teenagers and they seemed to have a lot of questions and questions I didn't have the answer to. So on my way home I wrote this poem. Some questions we don't know the answer to and probably never will. They really aren't important in our life. It's how we live that's important.

All Brothers and Sisters

I have met people from far across the sea,
    they are really not that different than me.
As I reached out to shake their hand
    though they were from another land,
There are brothers and sisters to me.

All Brothers and Sisters

I was also thinking of the people I've met from foreign lands. They aren't that different from me. Their thoughts and dreams, their wants and needs are pretty much like mine. Since I was a little girl I've thought we were all brothers and sisters anyway. Turns out it seems that's exactly what we are based on what we know about the science of genetics. We are all brothers and sisters, or at least cousins.

Sister of the Universe

My sister of the universe with eyes of crystal blue,
    the heavens all look down and smile
    as I write this song for you.
A voice so soft that speaks of truth,
    and words that set me free.
Sisters of the universe, forever we will be.

In the daily lives we live with the spirit we possess,
    all the universe responds
    if it's love that we express.
With each passing day we'll grow
    in wisdom and in truth,
    the ages cannot hold us
for we'll have eternal youth.

The power of the universe to which we have the
key,
    our mind and soul cannot be bound
    for love has set us free.
Love is really all we need to open every door.
    It's the power of the universe,
now and forever more.

Sister of the Universe
I had been shopping and had a car full of groceries. I
drove in and opened the car door and looked upward to
the sky and saw my sister's face as plain as day. I went in
and started writing My Sister of the Universe. I read it and
was surprised at what I had written.

I recorded it but have never sung it since. I say it as a poem. I did not write the music as it was written by Mike Lynch. His wife sang it with me on the recording. Many thanks to both of them. Great job!

We

We say, "I see"
　　but do we really see at all?
The beauty's there
　　it's everywhere
How much do you recall?

We take our pride
　　and so we hide
true feelings that are inside us.
　　When will we learn to be concerned
for others that are beside us?

If we deceive
　　and won't believe until it is too late,
I am concerned
　　when will we learn
love and beauty won't wait.

The Rebel

They call me a rebel
　　because I don't follow
the pattern that others have set.
　　I think my own thoughts,
I walk my own road,
　　so far I've had no regrets.

Where is it written
　　that I should live
my life like anyone else.
　　We're all born different
and that's reason enough
　　for me to be just myself.

My songs are all simple
　　and that's just exactly
the way I like them to be.
　　I never want
to confuse anyone
　　so I speak my mind truthfully.

You can live your life,
　　I can live mine
in peace and brotherly love.
　　We're brothers and sisters
here on the earth
　　and we pray to our Father above.

If we do the loving
    as he has taught us,
and just leave the judging to Him,
    In my opinion
we all could be happy
    and everybody would win.

The Rebel

A young man called and said he'd heard I was a song writer and the University of Washington at the New City Theater had people entertain between plays. He wondered if I'd come sing three songs at intermission and three more after the show.

I said I would love to do that. When I arrived I asked for him and when he saw how old I was, he didn't say it in words, but his reaction was "Oh my! She is old." I was then only 63 but I was often taken for about 45.

He said, "These are college students."

My reply was, "I'm here and if they throw tomatoes at me I'll leave." He still seemed to not want me to go on.

However, when I performed "Please" and "Seattle Weather" they did not heckle me. They were a wonderful audience so I told a little story thinking that would count as my third number. They stood, applauded, whistled, shouted and would not stop. I thanked them 3 times.

The MC, the one who did not want me to go on said, "We've never had anything like this. You are going to have to sing another song."

I sang another and after intermission I sang 3 more. Again they would not stop until I sang another song. That's where I learned to be happy and sad at the same time. Happy for me, sad for the person waiting to come on next.

At the end of the evening people were standing in line to shake my hand. One young man shouted, "You are a rebel!" He was so excited about it, I thought it must have been a compliment. So I replied, "Thank you very much."

On my way home I kept thinking a rebel? Everything I've done in my career has been unorthodox. So I'm a positive rebel, and I wrote the song on the way home.

Love is the Answer

If we could just erase the greed
That destroys all mankind,
In its place put kindness
And love within the mind.

There are so many ways to learn
And many ways to teach,
You don't have to shout
You don't have to preach.

I believe by showing
You accomplish so much more,
It's for certain if we love
We'd put an end to war.

The Encouragement Song

When you get a compliment
    it gives you encouragement
to help you along the road.
    The one you never see, until it will be
the one you never know where it goes.

Start with the little stuff
    sometimes it is enough
To get you where you want to go.
    Never underestimate
your ability to concentrate
    and the fun you will find as you go.

So don't tell me, my friend
    that you're at the end
and you don't know what to do.
    With all the opportunity
it would surely be lunacy
    to admit you quit 'for you're through.

If You Are Grateful

If you are grateful for the blessings
    that you have received,
Then show a little kindness
    for those who are in need.
Just look around you here and now
    there are many with no homes,
Think about how they must feel
    in desperation and alone.

If you've been blessed
    then you can share,
Show your brother that you care.
    It may just take a helping hand,
Someone like you to understand,
    To give them hope to try again,
So they like you
    can also win.

If you are grateful for the blessings
    that you have received,
Then give and share to help a lot
    of those who are in need.
What about the children
    who have no one to care,
Surely you can't turn away
    and leave them standing there.

If you are grateful for the blessings
    that you have received,
Then please give all you can.
    I really do believe
That with a little help
    from you who have a heart,
Today is the day to make a difference
    so let's start.

How can you hear a cry for help
    and turn and walk away?
Have you ever thought
    it may be you who cries one day?
It's America, the Land of Opportunity.
    Let brotherhood begin today
    with you and me.

In This World

I would like to thank you for the life you've given me
    and the kindness you have shown.
Every day is wonderful. It's pleasant as can be
    in this world you made that I call home.

I would like to thank you for all the things you give
    and the happiness I've known,
The piece and contentment many happy hours
    in this world you made that I call home.

I would like to thank you for the flowers I enjoy
    oh, how pretty they have grown.
The birds and animals to enjoy every day,
    in this world you made that I call home.

Life, The Question

The road that I was walking
    lay clearly straight ahead.
I was so sure which way to go,
    now doubts run through my head.
I cannot understand
    why can't we all be free?
Life that seemed so simple
    is now confusing me.

The pieces to the puzzle
    don't seem to fit at all.
The answer to the questions
    I simply can't recall.
Nothing seems to be the way
    it really ought to be.
Life that seemed so simple
    is now confusing me.

Things that were familiar
    are different now and strange.
It seems somewhere along the way
    that time has rearranged.
I'm in a situation
    I never thought I'd be.
Life that seemed so simple
    is now confusing me.

It seems like I am living
   in a place I don't belong.
I'm at a loss to figure out
   how to correct the wrong.
It really is bewildering
   and yet no one can see.
Life that seemed so simple
   is now confusing me.

Life, the Question

I wrote this because of what a young man asked after a
concert. He said, I'm confused and I don't know what to do.
On the way home these two poems:
Life the Question and Life the Answer (next page), came to
me in response to his statement.

Life, The Answer

I'll continue down the road
    until my vision clears,
And I can see the picture
    that's puzzled me for years.
The truth that lies within
    has enabled me to see,
Life is now so simple
    since love has set me free.

I have found the answer
    that I knew all the time,
Now I face reality
    there's peace within my mind.
At last I am the person
    I always knew I'd be,
Life is now so simple
    since love has set me free.

Everyone is asking
    what can the answer be?
I will gladly tell you
    it's simple as can be.
The power of the universe
    part of which is me,
Life is now so simple
    since love has set me free.

Father

Father, I'd like to talk for awhile
    to tell you I'm grateful
    for being your child.
To thank you for each day that I live
    and for all of the blessings you give.

He reached out his hand.
    He touched me and said,
    "When I was hungry, thanks to you I was fed.
When I was cold, you took me in.
    When I was lonely, you were my friend.
The love in your heart, you gave willingly.
    So I'd like to thank you for giving to me."

I stood in amazement
    and could not believe.
These words that he spoke
    were so hard to conceive.
I said, "Father, when did I do these things.
    I'm not an angel, I don't have wings."

Then he said, "My child it's so plain to see.
    If you've done it to others,
    then you've done it to me."

Thank You

I love you as a person
    I love you as a friend.
I believe that you,
    helped my heart to mend.
There is an innocence about you,
    that all people should possess.
You restored my faith,
    and added to my happiness.

Thank you,
    for the kindness shown to me.
Thank you,
    I hope that you can see,
I admire you
    as a person
I love you
    as a friend.
Let me thank you,
    once again.

You help so many people
    in this life from day to day.
With everything you do,
    and all the things you say.
You have a special way
    of turning grey skies into blue.
You make this world a better place,
    just by being you.

There must be many people,
    that feel the way I do.
Like me, you've touched their lives,
    and helped them start anew.
Your gentle kind and loving ways,
    are possessed by very few.
I wrote this song and sing it now,
    especially for you.

Thank You

I would advise people to always be grateful and thankful to the people who help to make their life pleasurable. It's something that each and every one of us should try to do to make people feel happy that have helped us.

Child of God

Judge me if you will
    it matters not to me,
for I am not your servant
    and I will never be.
I only have one master
    my Father, God above.
I am not a child of man,
    I am a child of love.

Man is ever seeking
    to try to take control.
He strives to dominate my mind,
    he wants to own my soul.
Man would have me bow to him
    instead of God above,
But I am not a child of man,
    I am a child of love.

You've heard that it is written,
    "The truth will set you free."
No more will you be bound
    by man's hypocrisy.
If God's your only master
    with no one else above,
Then you will be a child that's free;
    you'll be a child of love.

My Father is my God and Jesus Christ, his son
    Will be the one to judge me
when my life is done.
    The final say will not be man's,
 It's up to God above.
    For I am not a child of man,
I am a child of love.

Man should not sit in judgment,
    It says so in the Book.
Living life for one another
    will be what it took,
To show your true devotion
    be you Hindu, Moslem or Jew
For the one that has created me,
    also created you.

Made in the USA
Charleston, SC
06 October 2012